A Highly Sensitive Person's Life

Stories & advice
for those who experience
the world intensely

Kelly O'Laughlin

CONTENTS

Introduction

Welcome! If you are reading this, then you probably identify as a Highly Sensitive Person or know someone who does. I'm glad you're here.

Let's start with THE LIST. If you are a Highly Sensitive Person...

- You're overwhelmed easily. By things like noise, smells, light, and emotions.

- You're more emotionally reactive than those around you. You have more empathy and feel more concern for the struggles of others.

- You analyze information thoroughly and have difficulty making decisions. And you can't stop thinking about "wrong" decisions you made.

- You hear the phrase "Don't take things so personally" or "Why are you so sensitive?" a lot.

- Caffeine affects you strongly.

- You startle easily.

- You are strongly affected by violence and gore in movies, TV, and in the news.

- You don't thrive under pressure. Being told to do something in a short space of time does not energize you.

- You are often profoundly moved by music, art, and nature.

- You're observant to details. You can immediately identify what's new about a situation, what's changed in a room, or what's different about your friend's hair.

If this sounds like you, then we have a lot in common.

I wrote this book because I want to help people learn about high sensitivity. This information can help you better understand yourself and your loved ones. It can allow you to see yourself in a completely different light. **It can even change your life.**

The content of this book includes observations and personal stories that reflect aspects of my highly sensitive personality. I cover topics like sudden noises, stagnant air, feeling weighed down by plans and deadlines, caffeine, weather, relationships, and avoiding scary movies. You can find a lot of similar content at my blog, highlysensitiveperson.net.

My goal is to both entertain and inform; sometimes I offer tips on how to deal with the challenging aspects of being an HSP, other times I just rant and complain. There is no continuity, so feel free to jump around to sections that interest you.

My hope is that you will see yourself in some of my stories and realize the following:

"I didn't know this was part of being highly sensitive...now I don't feel so alone."

"I didn't know anyone else felt that way!"

"I'm not crazy!"

What does it mean to be a Highly Sensitive Person?

Highly Sensitive Person is a term coined by researcher Dr. Elaine Aron, the author of books like *The Highly Sensitive Person* (1996) and *The Highly Sensitive*

Person in Love (2001). So much of what I've learned about HSPs comes from her writings and research.

High sensitivity is a temperament, like introversion. It's innate—hardwired in your brain, like being left- or right-handed. **Sensitivity isn't an illness, a detriment, or a problem. It isn't something that needs to be fixed, cured, or suppressed.**

And, most importantly, **being sensitive doesn't mean you are weak**.

Here's a simple way to describe it: **Being an HSP is like experiencing all sensations and emotions ten times more intensely than other people.**

Being highly sensitive isn't wrong. It's just as valid as *not* being highly sensitive. In fact, sometimes it's beautiful.

If you aren't sure if you are an HSP, take the test at Dr. Aron's website at hsperson.com.

Knowledge is empowering

Realizing that you are highly sensitive is a piece of information that can change your life.

When I first learned about it, a weight was lifted from me. I was amazed to discover that I wasn't the only person who felt this way. I wasn't wrong or weird. My feelings all made sense when viewed through the lens of someone who experiences the world more intensely. For the first time in my adult life, I stopped wishing I was different.

I'd wasted so much time hating the way I was and wishing I could be *normal*. It was a relief to learn that I *was* normal; it's just that the *understanding* of HSPs isn't mainstream yet.

Who this book is for

- Those who identify as a Highly Sensitive Person.
- Those who think they may be a Highly Sensitive Person.
- Partners or loved ones of Highly Sensitive People who want to learn about the trait.

Who this book isn't for

This book isn't about scientific studies or research on high sensitivity. If that's what you're after, you'll need to look elsewhere.

Also, if you've thoroughly read my blog and listened to my podcast, then you've already heard my take on most of the concepts here.

A note about introversion

I often discuss topics related to being an introvert because most HSPs (70%) are introverts, including me. In some instances, these two traits seem intertwined, and it is difficult for me to differentiate between my high sensitivity and introversion.

If you are one of the 30% of HSPs who is an extrovert, please keep in mind that some of my introvert observations might not resonate with you.

A note about social anxiety

High sensitivity and introversion are not social anxiety. All three are often confused. It's true that many HSPs and introverts have degrees of social anxiety, but not all. I frequently see memes or quotes on social media about how introverts always want to be alone and hate being around people or going outside. That isn't introversion—that's social anxiety or phobia or asocial behavior.

It bugs me when these traits are confused, but in the end, defining them exactly and perfectly isn't the point—what matters is how they apply to you and your life and happiness.

And one more note...

You'll notice that I reference my husband Jim frequently. He is an extroverted, non-HSP. It is helpful for me to consider his points of view because he processes things so differently than I do.

And...Here are some bonuses!

I've put together some bonuses for you, including:

- A mega-list of products I love for HSPs & introverts.

- A colorful, mini-ebook of my top travel tips for HSPs.

- A list of my top 5 favorite HSP Podcast episodes.

Just head to highlysensitiveperson.net/bonus to pick up these extras.

Chapter 1

The Trait of High Sensitivity

Why is sensitive seen as weak?

By definition, sensitive means *quick to detect or respond to slight changes, signals, or influences.*

That doesn't sound weak at all—it sounds observant. It sounds like someone I want to be friends with!

Being sensitive means you are very aware of other people's feelings and thoughts, your own feelings and thoughts, your environment, animals, art, music, and everything around you.

So, then, why the heck did *being sensitive* become a bad thing?

Equating *sensitive* with *weak* is what many of us were taught from pop culture and the people around us; it's what we grew up with—and that's a shame. We are taught that sensitive = sissy. *Get a thicker skin. Suck it up. Quit whining.*

But that belief is wrong and needs to be unlearned.

Sensitive people are the artists, the musicians, the nurses, the teachers, the philanthropists, the counselors. They are nurturers, leaders, and inventors. They are politicians, entrepreneurs, and CEOs. Being sensitive is a wonderful quality.

The only downside, sometimes? Being the bearer of the weight of being sensitive.

7 tips for coping with the challenges of high sensitivity

Have you ever said to yourself: *I'm tired of being hurt and let down by others. How can I be less sensitive?*

Maybe you feel like you give a lot to other people but they don't return your thoughtfulness. You care so much, but others don't notice. You can't trust many people because they will inevitably hurt you or let you down. Your empathy weighs heavily on you. It's all so tiring. How can you deal?

Try this handy phrase: **Acknowledge, accept, and adjust.** When something is bothering or affecting you, don't ignore it—**acknowledge** that it's happening. Don't beat yourself up about it; **accept** that your reaction is a natural part of who you are. Then, think about what you can **adjust** in your life and attitude to better cope with these challenges.

Here are some strategies that may help.

1. **Remember, *you* are the only one who can make *you* happy.** Think about the way you talk to yourself in your head. Are you nice? Or are you critical and unforgiving? *Would you talk to other*

people the way you talk to yourself? Be gentle. Give yourself a break. Being compassionate and empathic to the world comes naturally; learn to apply that same compassion to yourself.

2. **Don't impose your expectations on others.** We're human; sometimes we let each other down and hurt each other. Realize that while you may be highly perceptive and considerate, *you can't expect everyone to be that way.* And that's okay. Learn to enjoy your own journey and don't expect others to understand or even be able to share in the way you experience the world.

3. **Identify the things that drain you and avoid them (within reason).** Maybe you are drained by watching violent or emotional TV shows or movies, being around certain people, hot/cold weather, incessant noise, bright lights, whatever. Figure out what reduces your energy and find a way to lessen the amount of time you spend doing it.

4. **Identify the things that energize you and <u>do them regularly</u>**. Maybe it's reading, meditation, running, volunteering, or spending time with pets or human friends. Acknowledge the healing power of these activities and don't neglect spending time doing things you enjoy.

5. **Set boundaries**. Sensitive people often have a hard time saying "no." Giving too much of yourself to others can suck your energy dry. Realize it's okay to say "no" or let things go.

6. **Talk to a sensitive friend or family member**. It helps a lot to have someone who understands.

7. **When you are down, consciously choose to focus on things that lift you up**. Remember moments when your happiness is amplified: maybe it's trying a new recipe, playing with a puppy, volunteering, or sending someone a thank you letter. When you are feeling hurt and down, don't retreat to a dark room to ruminate alone. Consciously make the choice to do something that will raise your mood.

How to calm down when you are obsessing

While there are many positive aspects to being highly sensitive, sometimes it can be tiring and, well, painful. We might not be able to control our sensitivity, but we *can* try to adjust our reactions to things.

I'd like to share a tactic that has helped me: **Try to "catch" yourself when you find yourself obsessing or getting worked up over something.**

Let's say your boss says something critical to you. Or you say something awkward to a friend.

You find yourself getting worked up. What did your boss mean? Is he mad at you? What if your friend was offended or hurt by what you said? Then you obsess over it. All. Damn. Day.

When I find my worry growing and spiraling out of control, **I try to realize and acknowledge that it's happening.**

I stop and think to myself, "Hold on, Kelly—you know that you sometimes over-think things. Maybe this isn't as bad as you're making it out to be. What's the worst that could come out of this situation? Is it really worth putting yourself through all this worry?"

So what if my boss said something critical? Maybe he's having a bad day. And if I made a mistake at work? He'll get over it. We all make mistakes. He's not going to fire me over it.

If I accidentally said something mean/awkward to a friend? What's the worst that could happen? Maybe it wasn't so bad. She'll get over it. There's nothing I can do about it now.

It's a strange feeling to doubt your own natural responses. Your reactions to the world are how you deal with...well, everything. If you can't trust your own reactions, then what can you trust?

Our perceptions are still valid and good, but they may be more intense than most other people are used to. It helps to acknowledge that and save our intense reactions for times when it is more appropriate and useful. Like a secret superpower!

Worrying about worrying: anxiety management

Not every Highly Sensitive Person struggles with anxiety, but many of us do.

We've all heard of anger management—but what about anxiety management? Anger management teaches people how to understand and acknowledge their feelings and anger. For us anxious folks—we can apply the same principles to teach ourselves to acknowledge when we are heading down the rabbit hole of anxiety and worry.

When we feel anxiety coming on, we often rack our brains to find reasons for the symptoms, hoping that we can figure it out and **solve it**. But, often, the source of our heightened emotions isn't real, so our brain goes in a circle of worry, trying to find the source of the worry when there isn't one! We *invented* it.

There have been times I've tried to explain my anxiety to my husband, and he's said, "Let me get this straight: **you are worrying about worrying?**" And I can't help but laugh, because he's right.

So, how to manage anxiety?

When you feel panic coming on, try to ignore it. Acknowledge what is happening and don't let it grab on to you. I know this is easier said than done. Once you decide to ignore it, then realize that you need to find a way to relax, immediately, before it sinks its hooks into you.

I tell myself something like, "Okay, my mind wants me to freak out right now, but I don't want to let it happen because I hate the way it feels." Then I focus on taking relaxing breaths and trying to find something to distract myself. I will remove myself completely from the situation.

Sometimes I will put on a mindless TV show. Or, I will tell Jim, "I'm feeling anxious and starting to freak out. Please help!" And he will either help me take my mind off it or we'll talk about what's worrying me, and he'll explain things though his non-anxiety-addled brain. It helps a lot to have someone who understands.

Decision-free living

Do you realize how much energy decision-making takes from you over the course of a day?

Let's look at how HSPs approach decision-making. We thoroughly examine and sometimes research every aspect of a decision's outcomes. This careful weighing of options isn't easy. Plus, we hate regret. **Making a bad decision is like a mini-failure.**

For me, deciding *what to eat* takes a lot of decision power. I love to eat at restaurants; it's one of my favorite things to do. However, I want to be healthy, not gain weight, and not spend too much money. The daily internal battle between ordering a giant burrito or munching on carrots takes a lot of energy. Do I eat what I crave, or something that's good for me?

What if I didn't have to make that decision every day?

As it turns out, it just takes some willpower and planning ahead. It's easy to find weekly meal plans online and in cookbooks. I have decided that my goal is to choose a meal plan (well, okay, that's one decision), prepare all the food ahead of time, and stick to it for a full week.

With just a little extra preparation, and yes, a decision or two, I can avoid the daily mental battle about what to eat. This feels exciting to me.

Here are some other daily decisions that might bog you down:

<u>Exercise</u>. I hate working out, but I know I have to do it. Sometimes I bargain with myself. "Well, I took a long walk today—maybe I don't need to go to the gym," or, "I will skip the gym today but exercise really hard tomorrow."

The solution? I choose a gym that's extremely close to my home or workplace. This gives me less of an excuse to skip it. Also, try a quota system. Tell yourself that you have to go the gym X times per week. This works for me, because it gives me the power to choose which days I skip.

<u>What to wear</u>. I put a lot of thought into my outfits. Not because I'm stylish—ha, no. It's because I don't want to be caught unprepared. I check the weather forecast every day and dress appropriately. If I know I'll be walking a lot, that means comfortable shoes, and comfortable shoes are usually sporty, which means I have to wear a sporty outfit. If I'll be outside in the sun, I want to wear a hat, which also affects the rest of my outfit.

My solution? Owning fewer clothes = fewer decisions. Spend more for timeless, stylish, quality items that are multi-functional and don't wear out. If you have less to choose from, that's less energy spent deciding what to wear. Steve Jobs and Mark Zuckerberg are famous examples of people who've adopted a "uniform" to avoid the decision power required in choosing daily outfits.

Whether or not to go to a social event. 70% of HSPs are introverts, which means that social situations can use up a lot of our energy. I like hanging out with my friends, but after a few hours, I'm spent. I feel guilty about not wanting to attend some social events. I don't have a legitimate reason why I don't want to go, other than just *not feeling like it.*

My solution? Make a quota system for the week or the month. Plan that you will go out X times per week. If you've already attended your quota for the week, then you don't have to feel bad about skipping an event. If you have open-minded friends, you could even tell them about your quota system so they understand why you turn them down. (Sorry guys; I hit my quota!)

Should I buy . . . ? I like to strike a balance between being frugal and knowing when to treat myself. If I find something I like but don't *need*, I spend too much time going over every aspect of the purchase in my head. Is it worth it? Will I wear/use it a lot? What else could I buy with that money?

The solution? Walk away. If I'm still thinking about the item a day or two later, that's a good indication that I truly do want it, and maybe it's worth a splurge. If I forget about it, then it's not that important after all.

Searching for the
stasis of peace

I'm learning every day how to better manage my needs as a person with high sensitivity and introversion. Sometimes I feel frustrated and mad at myself because I have to do so many things that aren't "normal" just to feel comfortable. I wish so many little things didn't bother me. But they *do*, and that's just how it is.

One day, I realized that I'm always searching for a **stasis of peace.**

By this, I mean: **I try to design my life so I am in the most comfortable situations possible to avoid anxiety, stress, and panic.** Since I know I can't change how I am, I have to plan my life the best I can. Right?

I attend fewer social events (and I don't beat myself up about it). When I do attend social events, I limit how many hours I'm there. I never watch horror movies. Jim also understands how I feel and is understanding. I work for myself from home, which has eliminated a ton of stress from my life (although it has its own set of problems). Overall, I am happier and freer from stress than I used to be.

But is this sustainable? Is this reality?

Sort of.

I've learned that **I can't expect to build a world around myself that fits exactly into what I think are my needs**. Trying to make the world into my ideal will only lead to disappointment. Plus, I'd waste a lot of energy building the *bubble* that I'd live in, struggling to keep it together.

The *stasis of peace* is a delicate balance. I can try to build my life so I am respecting my temperament, but I also must acknowledge when I start to feel bothered or upset, accept it, and **relax into it.**

Do some sounds fill you with rage? Maybe it's misophonia

Are there certain sounds that trigger extreme annoyance and anger in you?

It could be chewing, footsteps, sniffling, throat clearing, keyboard clicking, crinkly food wrappers, smacking lips, certain words or letters, slurping—or any sound, really.

If this sounds like you, perhaps you have misophonia: A decreased tolerance of sound.

Highly Sensitive People are more sensitive to the world around them, so it makes sense that misophonia could be a crossover symptom that some HSPs experience.

"Misophonia is a selective sound sensitivity which means you really, really hate certain sounds," a misophone acquaintance, Vivienne, told me. "Particularly anything to do with the mouth. Crunchy wasabi peas and loud breathing are big triggers for me. Sometimes even the sight of people eating can activate it."

And the reaction can be severe. She says that some triggers make her feel "trapped, invaded, tight in the chest, really anxious and sometimes extremely angry. Sometimes it's so bad I have to escape and have a little cry."

One Reddit user wrote, "I can't stand the sound of gum chewing or nail biting. It literally makes me want to punch someone, cry, scream, crawl out of my own skin."

Misophones often find that they need to structure their lives around the disorder. Working in a cubicle was difficult for Vivienne due to the aural triggers that inevitably arose. The triggers can distract and anger to the point where focusing on work is impossible. Eventually, she struck out on her own to work for herself; now she can better control her environment.

How do people deal with misophonia? There is no cure—not even a treatment. The disorder is not well studied, but awareness is growing. It seems that most misophones aren't without a good pair of noise-canceling headphones. Getting enough sleep, exercise, meditating, and maintaining a good diet are helpful.

If you think you have misophonia, know that you aren't alone. For support, check out reddit.com/r/misophonia and the Facebook

misophonia support group at
facebook.com/groups/misophoniasupport.

Chapter 2

Personal Stories & Realizations

This chapter is a compilation of my personal experiences as an HSP. I rant, rave, and occasionally offer some insight.

How did being a highly sensitive introvert affect you as a child?

When you look back at your life, can you recall any memories where you were made to feel guilty, inadequate, dumb, or unsuccessful about being highly sensitive or introverted?

As a child, I remember being told to *speak up, participate more, go play with the other kids, stop being so shy*, and *get your head out of your book*.

I hated class participation. I would do everything I could to avoid the teacher's eyes when he or she was scanning the classroom, looking for someone to call on.

In 5th grade, I remember not wanting to participate

in Recess. I was bored by it. It was forced socialization and anxiety for me, as someone who only had one or two friends. I asked the teacher if I could stay inside the classroom and read instead. I remember sitting alone in the classroom with my book, surrounded by empty desks, so happy, while the other kids played outside. I didn't think what I was doing was that weird; I thought all the *other* kids were weird. My teacher called me a "little introvert"—can you believe I remember that? I didn't even know what it meant.

I also remember a class field trip to a roller skating rink in 6th or 7th grade. I didn't want to go. It sounded stressful, tiring, and like a lot of anxiety over being *popular* and *cool,* which are the most important things in the world to a 12-year-old. I think my mom gave me a note asking if I could stay at school instead. I remember I sat all day long in the counselor's office, reading books about ancient Egypt (which I was obsessed with at the time). I faintly recall the teachers treating me like I was weird. It made perfect sense to me, though: why would I go on the roller rink field trip if I didn't want to?

In retrospect, I am grateful that my parents didn't force me to go. They are introverts, too. Maybe they understood. Regardless, I can look back now and laugh about what a weird kid I appeared to be.

I played sports from a young age, particularly softball

and basketball. I was good at softball through high school, but my basketball career ended early, and not just because I was short. I didn't have the personality for basketball. It's a supremely team-oriented sport, and one where you need a lot of confidence.

I remember my basketball coach saying that we players should always think, "*I want the ball.*" I always thought, "I do *not* want that ball. I might mess up."

I was awesome at defense because that was easy; I was fast. But on offense, I would subconsciously run to parts of the court where I knew I wouldn't be passed the ball. If I did get it, then I wanted to get rid of it as soon as possible. I was too nervous about messing up and being embarrassed.

You might be wondering: What does being unconfident about basketball have to do with introversion or high sensitivity?

I was timid because I analyzed everything—paralysis by analysis. It's not that I couldn't physically perform like the other girls. I feared that I would always make the wrong decisions and let down my teammates and coach. If I could have relaxed and thought less, I believe I would have performed better.

Tennis became my best sport. Why? Because it's more individual. There was less pressure because I didn't have to worry about letting someone else down.

The panic of hot, still air

Claustrophobia: Extreme or irrational fear of confined places.
Cleithrophobia: The fear of being enclosed.

I never identified as claustrophobic (or cleithrophic) before. But for some reason, over the past couple of years, I've come upon instances where I've experienced panic when I feel like I'm trapped in a situation or trapped in a place.

Here's one situation. Last year, Jim and I took a four-hour bus ride while traveling in Thailand. A few days earlier, we'd been on a huge, comfortable bus with awesome air conditioning. That trip was fine. So we assumed the next ride would be the same.

Wrong! We were packed over capacity into a minivan, with the air conditioning a tiny trickle of air—just enough that we weren't melting. There we sat, uncomfortable, with our sweaty legs sticking to the people next to us.

After the first ten minutes on this bus, I looked around and thought, "This is where I'm going to be for the next four hours." And panic started to rise inside me.

There was no way out. (Well, technically I could tell

the driver to stop and let me out, but then I'd be stranded in the middle of nowhere.) Realistically, I had decided to take this bus ride and I had to get through it. I thought about what would happen if I had a panic attack, and that made me feel even worse.

What got to me the most was the **heat and lack of air movement**. When I'm in a stuffy, warm room with no air movement, **I feel like I can't breathe.** Having a fan is essential when I'm ill, dizzy, or overheated.

This *trapped* feeling has happened to me twice on overnight train rides, too. On both occasions, the train windows were closed and there was no air circulation. As I laid on my hard sleeper bed on the train, with the bunk above me just inches from my face, the air was so close that I felt like I couldn't breathe. The panic was starting. On those occasions, I had to get up and walk around the train car while everyone else was asleep, in an effort to calm down.

One time, I ended up doing something Jim and I still laugh about. It was so hot and stuffy in the train and the air was so close that I felt suffocated. Time seemed to be standing still. **I simply could not bear it;** I had to do *something*.

In the middle of my long-suffering night, I pulled the sheet off my bed, took it into the (vile) train bathroom, then used the sink faucet to wet the sheet—all while everyone else was asleep. When I crept back to my bunk, I used the wet sheet to cool myself down. (Jim and I joked that the next day, the people who tidied up the train would be grossed out by my questionably wet sheet.)

To a non-HSP, I bet the wet-sheet thing sounds quite strange. But the still, close air was all I could think about. I had to do *something* or I was losing my mind.

By wetting the sheet, I gave myself the ability to change my environment in a small way. I could move the fabric around and feel the cool parts throughout the night. I had something to distract me from the utter stillness and the walls closing in on me.

The feeling of being trapped, without any control, is **completely terrifying** to me. I have definitely gained empathy for people who are claustrophobic.

The weight of commitment & schedules

If I have one thing to do, it weighs on me all day. Even if it's something enjoyable. There will be a kernel of anxiety in my brain all day, until the event happens.

For example: the other day I had a yoga class at 6:30pm. I was looking forward to it. But, for some reason, everything I did the rest of the day revolved around that class—in my head.

At 1pm, I thought: "I have five hours until the class." Even though five hours is a long time, and plenty of time in which to do things, I felt I couldn't get anything done until the class was over and out of the way.

Until the event or activity takes place, I can't truly engage in anything else.

The worst is if I have an early-morning flight. I will barely sleep all night. And if I do doze off, I'll dream about missing the flight. And if I have a flight in the evening, I will feel anxious all day, until I get to the airport.

On days where I have multiple engagements? Say, a noon dentist appointment and then a birthday party at night? I won't be able to get anything else done all day. I have too much going on!

Check out this scenario my mom described to me: She was a regular during the drop-in times at the local tennis club. One day, the club announced that instead of simply showing up to play, members now had to schedule themselves for drop-in time.

My mom instantly felt turned off. What she'd liked about drop-in tennis was that there was no obligation; she could decide to go anytime she felt like it. No commitment, no pressure. She didn't have to answer to anyone if she didn't show. And now that she felt she had to commit, she didn't want to.

As she explained this to me, I completely understood where she was coming from. It was a small loss of control.

This is also why I dislike working in a traditional office environment. At one job, I had to log in and log out of my computer when I took lunch, so my lunch times could be tabulated. I couldn't stand feeling like every minute of my day was being counted. **Being held to such a strict schedule made me feel trapped and controlled.**

HSPs don't like feeling controlled or overwhelmed.

Having a clear day with nothing to do is bliss. There's no stress, no obligations, and I can make my own decisions. Perfect.

Sudden noises make me jump

A bus screeched to a stop in front of me as I waited to cross the street. I grimaced and instinctively covered my ears. I turned to Jim and asked, "Didn't that hurt your ears?"

No, he said.

"Ugh. It literally *hurt* my ears," I said.

A few days later, we were walking down the street and a car passed by, breaking the silence with a loud horn HONNNNK! I involuntarily let out a small yelp and jumped a bit.

"Why did you yell?" Jim asked, a little annoyed.

"I can't help it." I said, sheepishly.

Just the other day I used a public restroom and the toilet flush was so ear-splittingly loud that I yelled and cursed like a crazy person. This has happened to me with restroom hand dryers, too. (Well, not the cursing part.)

So, yeah. I'm sensitive to sudden noise, loud noise, incessant background noise, and high-pitched screeching (like children screaming or squealing bus brakes).

I asked Jim what he thought of this and he said: "You jump when you hear any loud, random sound that's unexpected. Basically, **it's anytime anything unexpected happens to you**."

Interesting. Oftentimes, I'm thinking about something when sudden noises occur, so the noise jerks me out of my train of thought. I think that's why I'm jumpy. When someone would walk up to my cubicle at work and start talking to me, often I would jump, because I wasn't expecting it.

As far as I know, there's nothing I can do about this noise sensitivity. I can't prepare myself for unexpected jolts of noise, so I've gotten used to being the crazy lady who reflexively swears at flushing toilets.

I can't shop when people are waiting for me

I've never been able to go shopping with other people. Especially when someone is waiting for me.

There have been times when Jim and I are at the mall, and I need to buy something, and he's in a generous mood and tells me to take my time. Woohoo!

I'll start to excitedly browse the racks, but within a couple minutes, I can't help but feel a weight on me— **the weight of someone who is waiting.**

Even though he told me to take my time, I feel bad making him wait. Usually, I look around for a couple minutes and then I think: forget it. And I leave the store. I can't do it.

I'll meet up with him and grouch, "I can't shop when you are waiting for me!"

He says, "But I *told* you to take your time! You can't blame this on me!"

Me: "I know…it's not your fault."

How is this an HSP thing? HSPs take longer than most to make decisions. We weigh every possible piece of information. So making a purchase can take me a long time because I have to think about *everything*. And even the smallest inkling of being rushed wrecks it for me. I can't make a decision if I feel rushed. I also have empathy for the person waiting for me—it seems rude to make them wait.

Caffeine is my kryptonite

As I type this, I am sitting in a café, sipping a decaf, as the hipster baristas roll their eyes at my lameness.

I am ridiculously sensitive to caffeine. One cup of coffee can make me feel terrible for hours. But, like getting sunburns, I seem to forget my caffeine sensitivity, repeatedly. Every month or so, I have a cup and I regret it.

The other day, I went to a cafe and ordered an iced latte. *Not* decaf—living on the edge, baby! I sipped it slowly, yet I felt the effects quickly.

I hate how it feels. It's difficult to explain. It's like this nervous, anxious, awful feeling right in my chest. My hands feel shaky. I feel like I can't breathe as deep. I *do* feel more focused, though, and I'm able to work harder and faster for a while. If only I could have the benefits without the drawbacks!

So why does caffeine make us feel anxious and jittery?

Caffeine stimulates the central nervous system, causing our hands to shake. It also increases our heart and breathing rate, which is the same thing that happens when the *fight or flight* anxiety response kicks in.

Because HSPs are continuously in flight or fight mode, stimulants like caffeine might be too intense. We are stimulated enough already—it's our default state.

So, I just have to live with the fact that I can't be a coffee aficionado. I've accepted it and adjusted—now, I'm a tea drinker.

Scary or violent movies? NOPE.

When I was a kid, my parents didn't let me watch R-rated movies. So, of course, that meant I really wanted to watch R-rated movies.

I remember going to a friend's house for a sleepover, maybe in middle school. All us girls sat in the living room and watched the recently released horror movie Pet Sematary. I was excited to see my first R-rated flick!

And...I was terrified. The other girls didn't seem as bothered as I was. I hardly slept that night.

From that day onward, I stayed away from horror movies. They scare me too much. I'm too jumpy and get too engrossed. When I go to bed, my mind spirals out of control until I've convinced myself that someone has broken into my house to kill me.

This doesn't sound like the confession of a grown adult, does it? You'd think that once you hit 30 you'd stop being irrationally scared like a little kid!

I remember watching a fight scene in one of the Jason Bourne movies, and the sound of breaking bones, the blood, the violence—I felt overwhelmed and wanted it to be over. I still remember that moment in the movie theatre. I leaned over to Jim and said, "This is so violent!"

Like so many other aspects of being highly sensitive, I've learned to acknowledge, accept, and adjust. Violent or scary movies take me out of the *stasis of peace* I try to maintain. So, I simply avoid them. It's that easy. Plus, I don't think I'm missing much.

More on TV & movies: incontinuities and illogicalities

I was watching *Big Bang Theory* today. In the episode, Leonard was being sent on a trip to Switzerland to observe the Hadron Collider. The entire show was about Sheldon trying to convince Leonard to take him on the trip instead of Penny, since it had been Sheldon's lifelong dream to see the Hadron Collider.

While watching, I thought, "Why doesn't Sheldon just book a trip to Switzerland and see it on his own?" The entire premise was rubbish, in my mind. The episode was ruined.

This happens to me ALL THE TIME.

Of course, that show is a sitcom, and isn't meant to be totally realistic. But when something illogical happens in a movie or TV show, I have a hard time looking past it, especially if it is central to the plot. I just stop caring about what I'm watching.

What does this have to do with HSP? I get emotionally invested in what I watch. When there is an issue with the logic, my emotional investment feels wasted because the show writers didn't care

49

enough about me, the viewer, to make it believable.

Yes, we watch TV and movies to be entertained, but I need to be able to believe the premise, at least mostly. Otherwise, why should I waste my time and energy watching it?

Second-guessing decisions

"I'd like the spaghetti carbonara, please," I said.

As soon as the waiter turned his back, I was mumbling to Jim, "Darn it! I should have gotten the red sauce..."

This is so common with me. I regret probably 75% of my restaurant food orders.

Why does this happen? Because HSPs are cautious decision-makers who weigh every piece of information before making a choice. Sometimes it takes us longer than "normal" to make decisions. And I'm usually *still* weighing all the information even after the decision has been made!

Here's what's going on in my brain (and probably what's going on in Jim's brain) when choosing something to eat at a restaurant:

Me: Do I want pasta or meat? Will pasta be too filling? Should I get red sauce or white sauce? White sauce is so unhealthy. But I haven't had it in so long! Chicken or ham? Maybe I should get something less expensive. I want the chicken, but only if it's not breaded. I'll ask for no peppers. I should get something with more vegetables.

Him: They have steak! I like steak. Steak, please.

Weather & setting affect my mood

I grew up in a region where winters are snowy and freezing and summers are hot and humid. Now, I live in Southern California, which has arguably the best weather in the country. It's pleasant year-round, with little rain and temperatures that never approach freezing.

Jim says that I have a "five-degree comfort zone." I'm perpetually too hot or too cold. Anytime we go anywhere, I bring a sweater or long pants or shorts or an entirely different outfit in case the weather changes and I get warm or cold. In fact, at all times I keep a sweater, hat, and sunscreen in my car. I hate being caught unprepared.

Recently, I visited my small hometown in Michigan for the first time in a few years. It was the perfect time of year to visit: October. The trees were changing colors and the weather was crisp. I sat alone in my parents' big backyard and stared at the giant trees swaying in the wind, the same ones I stared at in my childhood, in silence. It was so beautiful, inspiring, and moving, and brought me a sense of peace and clarity that I'd *never* felt before. *I felt like writing a freaking poem.*

Until that day, I didn't realize that specific weather, like autumn, and physical setting was so important to me. Fall feels so darn *good*. It is comforting and relaxing, and not too hot or cold. It's cool enough to drink tea and knit and take long walks through crunchy leaves wearing a cozy sweater or hoodie. Hot weather makes me sweat and feel uncomfortable, and I don't like that.

But it's more about peacefulness, to me. I miss the peacefulness of autumn in my small hometown. There are no other sounds. No traffic, no music, no talking. Just the sound of the wind and leaves.

When I think of other occasions and places where I have experienced that peaceful quietness, I think of my visit to Japan last year. Classic Japanese culture values introspection, beauty, and peacefulness—as evidenced in traditional Japanese gardens, for example. I walked quietly through bamboo forests, poured water on shrines from wooden cups, and explored deserted temples. I loved it so much—the emphasis on peacefulness and reflection as real values.

Like a true social extrovert, Jim is bored by peace and quiet. It doesn't do anything for him, and he doesn't find value in it. It is hard for me to understand the way he feels, and I'm sure he feels the same about me—I'm excited by silence, for goodness' sake.

I remember gazing at a beautiful garden and koi pond and thinking: *I need this in my life*. But how? I'm going to try to visit more places that are quiet and peaceful. I need to remember how important this feeling is to me—how restorative it is.

HSP vs. non-HSP: The challah debacle

I think the following tale nicely illustrates the difference between an HSP and a non-HSP.

Jim and I were invited to a Rosh Hashanah dinner at a friend's house. She told us to bring two loaves of challah bread.

We went to the Jewish bakery and they told us there were three varieties of challah. Since neither of us is Jewish, we didn't know which to get.

I paused, already starting to think it through: should we buy the cheapest loaf, since we don't know which to get? Or since this is a special occasion, should we get the bigger one?

And before I could figure it out, Jim said, "That one." He picked the least expensive one; it looked similar to a regular loaf of bread but bumpy on top.

Then the bakery person asked, "Do you want it sliced?"

So, again, I started the analysis. Getting it sliced would certainly make it more convenient to eat. But what if it's not supposed to be sliced? Wouldn't it be smarter to leave it as-is and let the host decide? I thought the point of challah was to tear it apart...

Jim: "Yeah, slice it, please."

I turned to him and said, "Are you sure? What if it's not supposed to be sliced?" But it was too late.

As we walked out, I asked him many questions. What if we made a mistake? Our friend was cooking this big, special dinner. What if the bread was a big deal and we messed it up?

In the car, I googled *challah* and *Rosh Hashanah dinner* and found a site saying that the loaf is held in the air, a blessing is said, then pieces are torn or cut from it. OH NO! How can you hold up a bunch of *sliced* bread? We were going to ruin dinner!

Jim's response to all this? "They didn't tell us to get a certain kind of challah, so they can't be upset at us for getting the wrong one."

My response to THAT? "You're right, but...don't we owe it to them to do a little bit of research so we don't mess up their holiday dinner that they worked so hard to prepare? They were nice enough to invite us."

A few hours after going to the bakery, it hit me–this was such an example of being highly sensitive. I was being conscientious to a fault! I needed to **let it go**. As soon as we left the bakery, Jim was done thinking about the bread and was on to the next thing! Yet I kept turning it over and over in my head all day, worrying if we did the right thing or would mess up my friend's special night.

So, you want to know how dinner went, right?

No one cared about the sliced bread! All my worrying was for nothing. Typical!

Parties: Let's "get some drinks"

After going to a party, a group dinner, or hanging out with friends, extroverts will often energetically say: *Where are we going next?* They feed off the social energy.

Jim does this. We'll have had a lovely dinner with friends, we've paid the check and are ready to leave, and he says, "Let's go get some drinks!"

Meanwhile, I'm thinking, "Noooooooo!!"

When a group dinner is ending, I'm happy and fulfilled after having spent a nice time chatting with people I enjoy. And now it's time for the evening to end and go home. Everything is great at that moment; why do we need to prolong it? Why take a great night and beat it into the ground?!

I guess his thinking is, "Let's keep the fun going!" But my theory is that the longer you stay out, the less fun it gets.

There is a certain point at which everyone is settled in and the conversation is lively and fun. I'm having a great time! But from that apex, it can only go downhill. Someone will get tired. Or the group energy

59

starts running out.

Introverts like me frequently dislike hanging out at noisy, crowded bars or clubs. I believe that extroverts like "going out for a drink" because they think:

- It's fun to be around other people!
- I want to get out of the house / have a change of scenery!
- It's stimulating!

These things do not matter much to the introverted HSP. Well, I take that back–we *can* and *do* enjoy these things...

Sometimes,
and for brief periods.

If you have an extroverted partner that loves to go out, it helps to alternate your desires. Maybe one night you go out, and the next time you stay in, or go somewhere more low-key, or invite people over to your house instead of going out.

I've found that my sweet spot is just that: going to a friend's house or having people over to my place, drinking wine, and just talking. There's no loud music to make it difficult to talk, we are comfortable, and we don't have to worry about seating or parking or getting a bartender's attention.

What also helps is that everyone is getting older. Finally, Jim and our friends are catching up to my grandma-like ways. No one is itching to go bar-hopping all night or get hammered. I'm so glad those days are over.

So if you are an introverted, highly sensitive, young 20-something: hang in there. Eventually your friends will become more appreciative of low-key evenings just like you!

Parties: Taking breaks and leaving early

Jim and I went to a party at a *new* friend's house the other day. I'd never been to their place before. I knew hardly anyone at this party. That meant the dreaded *small talk*.

This party brought back old feelings of social inadequacy. The past few years, I'd done well at parties because they were full of people I already knew—people with whom I was comfortable. But now I was reminded that I am actually *not* good at parties.

It takes a massive amount of energy for me to put on the show that is *small talk*. But I do listen to people intently and try to have a good conversation. It's tiring.

After only an hour and a half, my thoughts drifted away from the people around me. I thought, "I can't do this anymore. I want to get out of here." But it was too early to leave.

I walked over to Jim and quietly said, "I'm going to go sit in the car for a while."

"That's weird," he mumbled, as he handed me the

keys.

As soon as I walked out the front gate into the dark, quiet night, I took a huge breath and felt awesome. I got into the car, put the seatback down, closed my eyes and thought about how happy I was to be able to take this break. I mentally patted myself on the back for having this great idea to come to the car!

After about 30 minutes, I rejoined the party. No one noticed I was gone, of course.

My little party-rest-in-the-car made me happy because it gave me some *control*. I didn't have to feel trapped at the party—forced to be social or to feel awkward about not being social.

The truth is that I'm disappointed that parties are so hard for me.

Jim is an extrovert and loves being around people, so we have to compromise. Sometimes I want to leave a party early, but he'll be having a great time. Or, perhaps I want to skip a social event altogether but he doesn't. What kind of partner would I be if I made him go alone? That's not very nice.

Gatherings became something I would dread because the night would often end in frustration—mostly at myself. Do I have a right to want to go home early? Enjoying parties is normal, right? So I'm the weird one because I want to leave early.

But then I'd think—that's not fair! My desires are just as valid as his. Me wanting to leave early is just as valid as him wanting to stay longer, isn't it?

Should I suck it up and pretend to have fun even though I am miserable, or can I bail? However, if we do leave early, I feel guilty that I made him leave when he was having fun. It's a problem with seemingly no solution.

But there is a solution. Take two cars.

It feels great to have an *out*. When we each drive separately, I have the freedom to leave when I want and he can stay as long as he desires. Plus, I don't have to feel guilty about making him leave early. Everyone wins!

The HSP superpower of smell

A few years ago, I was standing in my kitchen and I faintly smelled something. Something bad. I asked Jim, "Do you smell that?" He says no.

Now I'm on a mission. "I swear I smell something bad. Where the heck is that coming from?" I mumbled to myself.

If you are anything like me, you know what came next. I searched every single corner of the kitchen looking for this smell.

I ran the garbage disposal, sniffed over it, and used a disposal cleaner to make sure it didn't smell. I opened the dishwasher and sniffed around. I smelled nearly every item the fridge and the pantry, holding them to my nose to check for spoilage. I swept the floor to see if any food had fallen there. I cleaned the countertop and sniffed around the oven and stovetop.

I sniffed over every single thing in the kitchen. Where the hell was it coming from? I was losing my mind. (Of course, the whole time, Jim smelled nothing!) Eventually, I had to give up. Maybe the smell would go away. I lit some candles and tried to think about something else.

The next day, I went to heat up some leftovers in the microwave. I opened the door, and inside, *I saw raw chicken that I had put there to thaw. Two days ago.* That I had forgotten. So gross!

Now, you don't have to be an HSP to smell old, raw meat, but the point is that I *always* smell things that are spoiled before anyone else does. And in those instances, I will go on a rampage until I find the source of the stink.

This sensitivity to bad smells in the kitchen (usually from the garbage bin) led me to what might seem a strange habit to some: I put all perishable garbage in the freezer.

So, if I'm preparing carrots, the peelings go in a bag in the freezer. Empty yogurt cups, egg shells, containers that used to hold raw meat, banana peels—anything that could smell bad in the garbage goes into the freezer so it won't start to stink in the waste bin. Then we throw out the freezer bag on trash day. This practice has helped eliminate crazy stink searches.

But what about good smells?

Right now, the orange blossoms are out in full force in my neighborhood. They are absolutely intoxicating. When I walk by one particular orange tree, I am blown away by how strongly it smells. I stand there, smiling, with my eyes closed, just taking it in. And sometimes, after it rains, there is a faint scent of eucalyptus in the air. Any time I can pick up that scent, it feels special—calming and clean.

When I smell lovely things, like orange blossoms, eucalyptus, or garlic simmering in olive oil (another favorite), it is more than just a smell. It makes me *feel* something. It's like a moment of sensory bliss, and I just can't get enough of it.

The right to silence trumps the right to noise

Get ready for some rage!

I remember the time I heard someone playing music in their cubicle. It was several cubes away, but I could faintly hear it.

I worked in a cubicle farm, as it is affectionately called. Dozens and dozens of cubicles next to each other in a giant room. I remember sitting straight up, with a look of annoyance on my face, as I thought about what to do. I was a writer, and I needed silence to write. I could deal with the typical ambient noise of the office, but something like music distracts me. Because some person had decided they needed to hear some tunes, now I couldn't work.

Listening to music in a cubicle—when surrounded by dozens of other people in cubicles—is inconsiderate and selfish. The music player has made the decision that everyone else will now listen to her music, whether they want to or not. That is rude. Plus—why couldn't she use headphones?

I sat there in my cube, becoming increasingly

annoyed about this person's inconsideration. I debated with myself about what I should do. I told myself to ignore it, but I couldn't.

Finally, I got up and found the offender. I told her, nicely, that I was sorry but could she turn her music off because I couldn't work? She turned it off. I'm sure the second I walked away, she IM'ed all her co-workers, "OMG some crazy chick just came over and told me to turn my music off, wtf?!" I didn't care. I firmly believed I was in the right.

Some people like to listen to music when they work, or have the TV on in the background, or go to a cafe with ambient noise. Then there are people like me that prefer silence or white noise with no distractions.

All of these preferences are okay. However, we have to live and work together in this world.

This is how I see it: In the workplace, my right to silence trumps others' right to noise. Why? Because my silence won't bother people or distract them from their work. Others can wear headphones to listen to music. Their need for noise will bother me and distract me; my silence won't bother them.

So, in my mind, the right to silence wins!

People pleasers: I don't want to bother you

Do you say things like this a lot?

"I don't want to be a bother."
"Let's do what is easiest for you."

My whole life has been spent saying things like this. I am constantly worrying about annoying or inconveniencing other people.

I always thought it was a lack of self-esteem. I am most concerned with not bothering people when I think they are more important, more experienced, smarter, wealthier, or busier than I am. Who am *I* to bother *them*?

You know why I try so hard not to inconvenience people? It's to prevent them from feeling like I *did* inconvenience them. I'm so afraid that people will think I'm annoying or a bother that I'll go out of my way to make sure they *don't* feel that way.

People pleasers can also have a hard time saying *no*. "No problem!" is something they often say. "Sure, I can work late tonight." "Yeah, you can stay at my place." "I can babysit, no problem." "I can lend you some money."

If you have a hard time saying *no*, then you may become frustrated, burnt-out, resentful, or overwhelmed when you take on too many responsibilities.

And why do HSPs have a hard time saying *no*? Because they don't want the other party to think they weren't helpful. If you always say *yes*, then others can't say you never work late, that you aren't generous, that you never help out, etcetera. You're covered!

Don't stand over me while I'm working

HSPs generally perform poorly when being watched, and yeah, I can totally confirm this.

One of my old bosses would sometimes stand directly over me and watch me while I did things on the computer. It was so insufferable that I called him out on it. I think I said something sarcastic, like, "Are you really going to stand on top of me while I do this?" Or, "I can't do this if you are going to stand there and watch me." Fortunately, we had a pretty relaxed relationship so he wasn't offended. I think he found it amusing that it bothered me.

When someone like a manager or boss is watching me do something, I freeze up. I cannot perform. Then I fear that I appear incompetent, like I can't do the work, just because I'm nervous about being stared at.

At another job, three of us were stuffed into an office room meant for one person, each with our own desks. One day, we had move to a different room in the same building. So, the three of us had to figure out where to put our individual desks within the new room. The other two people wanted to face the window, whereas my only suggestion was that I didn't want my desk facing another person. It would give me so much anxiety to have someone staring at me all day.

My officemates were understandably happy that they got the window view without argument, and I got to face the wall like a crazy person.

A few months later, I expressed to my boss that I would rather work in a cubicle instead of the shared office. No one could believe that I would give up being in an office to have my own private cube. In a cube, I would at least have the privacy of knowing no one was looking at me. Just that tiny bit of privacy was so appealing. I felt like I could make it through the day more easily and be less distracted. And you know what? They were nice enough to move me to a cubicle.

Here's my advice: If you are unhappy in your work environment, don't be afraid to speak up. Your Human Resources department might actually be able to help you. However, don't be surprised if your co-workers and managers don't understand *why* you need what you need. Don't worry about what they think—just talk to HR!

If you can finagle a better working environment for yourself, that's all that matters in the long run. The embarrassment of having to ask for it will wear off.

My first dog

Jim wanted a dog. I absolutely did not.

I'd never owned or cared for a pet in my life—well, other than a goldfish. My dad doesn't like pets, so we never had one when I was a kid. I grew up not caring much for animals in the home.

Anyone who has a dog has a dirty house, I thought. I didn't want my nice floor getting scratched and my couch and carpet getting stained. And I was not interested in cleaning up an animal's waste. Gross.

But after a few years, I found myself softening up. And I took something else into consideration: Having a pet is supposed to lower stress. I imagined taking the dog to the park and running around, getting exercise, and having a ton of fun. It sounded kind of great.

But then, as per usual, I dwelled on the negatives. It would be a loss of freedom, and so much commitment—almost like having a kid. What if we wanted to go on a long trip? We couldn't. What if we wanted to go away for a weekend? We'd have to put the dog in a kennel, which is expensive. Speaking of expensive–doggie health care. What if it got really sick and we were faced with the decision of spending thousands of dollars to make it better or... not?

Getting a dog means you are setting yourself up for a crushing loss. Someday, it's going to die. Morbid, but true. But then again, they say it's better to have loved and lost than to have never loved at all, right? Or am I better off avoiding such pain?

And—let's be honest—I'm not the most flexible, laid-back person. When something messes up my plans, it bugs me. Having a pet means unpredictability. But on the other hand, maybe that would be good for me?

Perhaps all the hassle and expense is worth it. A lot of people get joy out of having a dog, maybe I would, too.

So, Jim and I fostered a dog. We figured that was the perfect way to test dog ownership without the commitment. Our foster dog was a one-year-old, white poodle mix weighing 14 pounds.

I felt so much empathy towards this helpless little creature. When we brought her home, she wouldn't sit or lie down. She stood next to me all the time. She barked and freaked out all night long. She was probably so scared and confused!

Every single part of this experience was new to me. It was like when a jungle tribe is discovered that doesn't have contact with the outside world, then the tribespeople are introduced to things like cell phones and indoor plumbing and zippers and they are blown away. That was me with the dog. I was blown away by basic dog ownership stuff.

These little creatures have to depend completely on us for their needs. That's so scary! I would have anxiety all day if I wasn't sure I was getting food and water and if I thought my caretaker was leaving forever anytime they exited the room.

We ended up adopting this adorable little dog. Are you surprised? We've had her for a year now, and she's come so far with her fear and anxiety of the world. I swear, she is highly sensitive just like me. An HS*D*.

The experience of fostering dogs (we fostered two more) and owning a dog has utterly opened my eyes to a whole world that was previously ignored by me. Having grown up in a home with a negative view toward dogs, it was shocking to discover this huge well of love and empathy inside myself. I feel grateful to be able to interact with these loving, loyal, and vulnerable creatures. It makes my heart feel like it could burst.

Appreciating the small things

I was at a café, about to work on my laptop, and I ordered a hot cocoa. After a few minutes, the barista—who was working alone—brought it to my table, very carefully set it down, and rotated it so the heart shape he'd created out of the foam was facing just the right direction.

The entire time he was doing this, I was slightly smiling, and when he finished setting it down, he looked at me with a smile, too. I was in a country where I didn't speak the language, so smiling was the easiest way to communicate.

A non-HSP probably wouldn't think much of this interaction. Coffee art like that heart isn't anything special, really. But the care with which he placed it on the table touched me in a small way. He put effort into making this little heart. Again, it doesn't *mean* anything—it's just the fact that someone put effort into doing something unnecessary, something they didn't have to do, something with a hint of whimsy and playfulness.

I appreciate the hell out of stuff like this. Anytime someone has given me an unexpected gift or done something thoughtful for me, it touches me greatly. I am blown away that someone would care about me enough to take the time, effort, and expense to do something *just for me*.

I pay attention to details and when people do things they don't *have* to do. This is one of those things that's a benefit of being an HSP!

Politeness

We HSPs not only have good manners, but we often notice when other people don't. If Jim and I are shopping and he asks an associate for help, then I don't hear him say *thank you*, I quietly hiss, "You didn't say thank you!" (And then I feel bad about being annoying.)

One of my pet peeves is when I am telling a story and someone interrupts me, and then they don't acknowledge that they interrupted me, or they keep talking and let my story remain unfinished. To me, that is incredibly rude and disrespectful. If I interrupt someone, I try to be careful to fix the situation. I'll finish my thought and then say, "Sorry, I interrupted you–what were you saying?" or, "Please finish your story," or, I will ask a specific question to show I was listening to their story and, in a small way, apologize for interrupting.

The reason HSPs are very polite is because we are conscientious and don't want to offend people. I think respect is important, and I don't want anyone to feel disrespected. I'm a big fan of the golden rule: I try to treat others as I want to be treated.

Eating outside is overrated

It gets very hot in New York in the summer. It isn't unusual to hit 90°F. When I lived and worked just outside New York City, my coworkers always wanted to eat lunch in the courtyard outside our workplace. Even when it was very hot and humid.

The reasoning? They were stuck inside all day and lunch was their one chance to escape and be outside. I understood that, but I also didn't want to sweat in my nice work clothes when an air-conditioned building was right next to me.

Does. not. compute.

On one occasion, I remember opening the door to the courtyard and it felt like air from a furnace hit me in the face. "You guys, it is super hot outside—are you sure you don't want to eat inside with the A/C?" came my whiny plea. No, they inexplicably *HAD* to be outside.

Then there were the **bees**. There was a bee problem in the courtyard at my job, and everyone knew about it. Why sit outside, sweating in a cloud of bees, when you don't have to? I guess other people aren't as bothered by the heat and insects as I am.

When I was a kid, my dad built a wooden picnic table for our front yard. I think the idea was that we would eat out there occasionally. I dreaded putting my legs under that table, wondering what spiders and bugs would be having their way with my ankles. I was always on the lookout for ants and flies around our food. Why can't we just eat *inside*, where there are no bugs? To this day, I dislike sitting on outdoor furniture that hasn't been recently cleaned. *Spiders!*

It's not just the heat and the insects. I'm also bothered by too-bright sun or not having sunscreen when the sun is shining on my face.

So, when I'm given the opportunity to eat or work outside, most of the time I'd prefer to be inside, where the environment is controlled and comfortable. A lot of HSPs love nature and would prefer to be outside, but I'm on the other end of the spectrum. I'm not a big fan of eating outside.

Empathy: feeling the physical pain of others

This story takes place last year, when Jim and I lived in northern Thailand for a few months. I was working alone in a cafe when Jim showed up and sat at my table. I wasn't expecting him, since he was out riding our rented motorbike to the train station to buy train tickets.

After he sat down at my table, he calmly said, "I need your help." Immediately, I sensed something was wrong, but I could tell he was trying to be calm for my benefit.

"I need you to help me clean up a little scrape on my leg," he said. I then noticed his shirt was dusty and he had dirt on his arm. I instantly knew he had an accident. Scooter accidents are common in Thailand, especially among foreigners like us.

We went back to our apartment, he showered, and we assessed his bodily damage. There were big wounds on his knees and scrapes all over his body. The back of his knee was turning black and blue.

Apparently, a truck pulled out right in front of Jim. Jim hit the brakes but his scooter tipped over and he fell off. The guy behind him, who was also on a motorbike, ran into Jim—which caused the most injury. Now, Jim was left hobbling around our apartment in a lot of pain.

When we were first assessing his injuries, my entire body was enveloped in a pain of its own. Seeing wounds on the body of the person I love made me hurt inside. My nervous system felt like it was in a state of emergency. When I think about it now, I can't put it into words. I don't know why I felt that way. Obviously, I don't want him to be in pain. But it's deeper than that.

I want to be clear—I didn't look at his knee then feel pain in my knee. It's not like that. I just felt a bad feeling throughout my body.

I remember many years ago, Jim and I were chasing each other around our apartment. The way it was laid out, you could run in a circle around the kitchen and through the living room, so sometimes we would chase each other in circles. I know—silly. Once, while running, he slipped on a rug and went crashing into the floor and the wall. I *instantly* started crying! Why? It surprised us both. I think it was because I was somehow involved in his spectacular wipeout. I felt so, so bad, even though he was fine.

Sensitive to physical violence: boxing's not for me

During that same stint in Thailand, we went to a Muay Thai fight. I'd never seen boxing or fighting in real life before, so I looked forward to a new experience. I know I am sensitive to violence on TV and in movies, so I wondered if seeing people hit each other would bother me. And yeah, it kinda did.

As I watched the fights, there were some weird thoughts going through my head, like:
"That guy has a friendly face."
"He looks like a nice person. I hope he's alright."
"I wonder if he hates fighting but does it for the money."
"Maybe the gloves make the punches not hurt so bad."

One guy completely overpowered his opponent. He punched him so hard and fast over and over that I wanted it to stop. It was terrible! I didn't like seeing someone get hurt.

I kept thinking about the fighters and how they felt. I leaned over and asked Jim if he felt bad for them or wondered what they were thinking. Not really, he said. He was simply enjoying the fight.

It's not really surprising that I don't enjoy watching physical violence, even if both parties are in on it. I just don't see what's fun or entertaining about watching people get hurt.

Empathy for other people's loss

HSPs pick up on the emotions of others. Pain and sadness can linger in our minds and bother us more than it bothers non-HSPs.

When thinking about an example of empathy for others' loss, what popped into my head was something I haven't thought about in over 15 years. It was interesting to examine it all over again in the lens of high sensitivity.

When I was in high school, the father of a classmate died in a tragic plane crash. I wasn't close friends with his daughter, but we were friendly and played on some sport teams together. Her father was well known in the community; everyone liked him. My family knew his family.

Our small community was devastated. When I heard the news, I remember lying on my bed and sobbing until I couldn't breathe. I thought about so many scenarios—the moment the mother found out, when she thought about how she'd tell the kids, the moment she told them, and how they were all heartbroken together. The unspeakable, raw pain. How can they even bear it? I thought of my classmate and couldn't fathom how she felt. It made me hurt so much to think about it, and *I kept thinking about it.* I wondered why no one else in my family seemed to be as bothered as me.

And even now, I feel like a jerk for talking about how this affected *me*, since obviously how I felt is unimportant compared to the pain felt by his wife and daughters.

My family went to the showing at the funeral home. I didn't want to go because I worried I would cry. I didn't feel I had the right to cry—I wasn't close enough to the family to be so strongly affected!

But I made it through the showing. I saw my classmate there for the first time since her dad died, and I hurt for her. I thought about the mundane things we do in a day—like taking a shower, putting on clothes, brushing our teeth, and eating a meal. She had to do all of those things that day, knowing she was going to her dad's funeral. How could she do it? How could she function with such a huge loss?

To me, her loss represented the loss I will have to face some day when I lose someone close to me. I worry about that. But what good does that do? None, of course.

In situations like this, I wish I could turn off my sensitivity. It didn't do me any good to feel so much pain and sorrow about my classmate's dad's death.

Anticipatory grief

Anticipatory grief is a grief reaction that occurs before an impending loss, typically, the death of someone close to you. It's not unique to HSPs, but for us, anticipatory grief can be intense. (Surprise!)

I've not yet lost anyone very close to me. I know that someday it will happen, and I fear how I will react. I fear the pain.

Now, to a non-HSP, or someone who doesn't experience anticipatory grief, this may sound silly. Why would I waste energy worrying about something I have no control over?

Dr. Elaine Aron says that she's noticed HSPs "look ahead" in many ways, especially to things they will have to cope with, including loss.

She gives an example of how, halfway through a vacation, she started feeling sad about its inevitable end. I experienced the same thing a few years ago. Jim and I went on a nice vacation for two weeks and I could barely enjoy it because I knew I'd be back at work in a few days. I was so annoyed at myself for feeling that way! I have a hard time enjoying life in the moment, without constantly looking forward.

And last year, when I adopted the first dog I'd ever

owned, I was already thinking about it *dying*! Dogs have short lifespans, so I knew I'd be taking in an animal to love and someday dealing with its death. I've cried multiple times thinking about it. (As I look at my little furball curled up next to me right now, there's a lump in my throat.)

Dr. Aron hits the nail on the head when she says that we HSPs think about the *emotional* hole that might be left by the person who dies. We try to mentally work out a way to reassure ourselves that we would be able to carry on, that we would be okay.[1]

She says one way to handle anticipatory grief is by imagining the grief through a glass door. We can see the grief outcome, but we are not living with it yet.

I need to try that.

---

[1] Source: http://www.hsperson.com/pages/2Feb13.htm

Chapter 3

Delving Deeper into HSP

Now that I've shared some personal stories and pet peeves about being a Highly Sensitive Person, here are some thought-provoking, hopefully helpful essays on exploring the trait further.

Are you a High-Sensation Seeker?

Along with introverts, extroverts, and HSPs, there are also High Sensation Seeking HSPs. (Elaine Aron calls them HSS/HSPs.) Apparently, HSS/HSPs are quite rare.

High Sensation Seekers seek out activities or behaviors that allow them to reach a high mental or physical arousal level. This does not necessarily mean a thrill-seeking activity like bungee jumping or skydiving; it can mean simply seeking out new experiences and craving excitement, novelty, and change. It's the urge to explore a new part of town, visit an exotic country, take classes about unfamiliar subjects—taking mental, emotional, intellectual, or physical risks.

What I like about the concept of HSS/HSP is that the

HSP part of the personality will be careful, plan things out, and research, laying the groundwork for the sensation-seeking side to do its thing—but in a calculated, safer way than jumping in blindly. The high sensitivity part allows the sensation-seeking part to have its arousal/risk/excitement, but *thoughtfully*.

But HSS/HSPs balance on quite the tightrope! They may crave stimulation and excitement but fear and avoid overstimulation. That's a tricky balance.

Another fascinating aspect of HSS/HSPs is how they desire to work. An HSP might crave a comfortable, familiar routine in their job, whereas an HSS might be bored doing the same thing every day.

Personally, I'm not sure if I'm an HSS. I do love to travel to "exotic" places—when I first arrive in a new country, I feel like I'm on a high. The possibilities are endless. I can't wait to explore, learn, and soak everything in. However, I'm worried that since I get easily overwhelmed, my introversion and sensitivity will force me to take it slow.

You can take the High Sensation Seeker test on Dr. Elaine Aron's website: hsperson.com/pages/HSStest.pdf

Highly Sensitive Extroverts

As I've made clear so far in this book, I'm an introvert. But 30% of HSPs are extroverts. I can't write about being an extrovert first-hand, so I surveyed several self-identified, extroverted HSPs to better understand their trait.

Extroverted HSPs walk a tightrope between desiring/requiring a certain level of social interactions and becoming overwhelmed. (Introverts, conversely, don't feel like our lives are missing something without lots of social interaction.)

As Wendy, an extroverted Highly Sensitive Person, explained: "I receive energy from other people. Being an HSP, I fully feel it and take it in! But I tire faster; after a long period socializing, I'm totally ready to be alone and peaceful."

Anne-Leena agreed: "It's challenging to balance the 'kicks' you get from social situations/travel/learning new things and the tiredness afterwards."

A main difference between introverts and extroverts is that introverts feel drained by social interactions, whereas extroverts are energized by those interactions. As extroverted HSP Shalini said, "If I go for more than two or three days without interpersonal contact, I feel like I'm missing something." (Whereas an introvert like me—I'm perfectly fine with not being around people for a while.)

Wendy said: "It seems that introverted HSPs are naturally shielding themselves from things that would bother or hurt them—crowds, dominant people, noise, too much socializing, chaos. Whereas extroverted HSPs are perhaps willing and able to take some of that in, tolerate it a bit more, and draw some excitement from it."

I totally get what Wendy is saying. I think I avoid some loud, busy, social events because I fear how it will make me feel. I anticipate that it will suck out my energy. Conversely, the extroverted HSP craves the social activity—but in a certain amount, not above their desired threshold.

Like typical HSPs, extroverted HSPs are highly sensitive to pain, caffeine, loud noise, empathy, and being overstimulated; however, they also enjoy large parties, like to meet new people, and have lots of friends.

I asked the extroverted HSPs: What is your biggest challenge? A few respondents said that even though they're extroverts, they need breaks from social activity—and their friends struggle to understand this.

Allen explained it like this: "My work colleagues couldn't understand...'Here's Allen, the life and soul of the office, but he doesn't want to go out on Friday night?' "

In regards to other challenges, Margie said, "People assume that I am tougher emotionally. I appear confident, and I am. However, I cry easily when I feel deeply about something that is important to me or if a situation has affected me emotionally."

I hope that extroverted HSPs, just like their introvert counterparts, can accept and acknowledge their temperament and adjust their expectations of themselves accordingly. Remember that none of us are weird or wrong—we just experience the world differently.

Feeling overwhelmed by beauty in nature and art

I had a creative writing class in college where we had to write poems in different formats. I was not interested in poetry, but I was interested in getting good grades so I worked hard on the assignments.

To this day, I remember a poem I wrote called *To the Cathedral Builders*. It was about how I feel bothered by seeing something beautiful and not being able to take it all in. No matter how long I stay and stare at a beautiful cathedral, for example, I can never appreciate it as much as it *deserves* to be appreciated.

I have experienced this feeling a lot. When there is a moment I know I am seeing something special, something I traveled very far to see, something someone worked very hard to build, or a stunning natural wonder, I want to linger and ponder it for a long time. I feel like it deserves my respect.

And I am so overwhelmed by its beauty that I want to take it all in, to remember what I'm seeing, and to preserve the feeling I'm experiencing at that moment forever, because that is the right thing to do.

But I can't.

No matter how long I stare, I can never save that exact feeling to recall again in the future. I can take photos and tell myself how important that moment is, but it is still a moment, and soon, it's gone.

In these situations, I've learned that I have to let go of the guilt and pressure I'm imposing on myself. I remind myself to simply enjoy the moment. **I appreciate it for what it is, and let it go.**

This happens to me frequently with flowers.

There are so many beautiful flowers in Southern California. Many times when I am out for a walk, I see a random flower—usually a perfectly symmetrical one—that captures my attention. When I see a flower like this, I exclaim to an uninterested Jim, "Look! It's so perfect!" and I can't stop looking at it and commenting on it. I wonder how he doesn't seem to care one bit! It's so amazing that the flower is so perfect.

He'll be like, "Yup. It's nice."

There is something about this perfection in nature that gets to me. It's like the ultimate beauty, and it seems like it's by accident. Now, I know nature isn't *by accident*—that flowers look the way they do to attract pollinating bees and stuff like that—but the way the flowers just grow and reveal their flawless designs is such a wonderful thing for us humans, because we get to enjoy it.

I did a web search for "why are flowers beautiful" and a random comment caught my eye.

"Bees and humans both have brains that are based on the same basic building blocks, neurons or nerve cells. These cells are linked together in networks that have predictable behaviors. First and foremost is threshold behavior. Stimuli must overcome a given amount of intensity before evoking a response. Plants have evolved flowers that evoke a response from neural networks. An interesting behavior in neural networks is their lack of sensitivity to the idea of too much stimulus. **You can't have too much beauty.**"[2]

Maybe I'm drawn to symmetrical, beautiful flowers because their intense beauty stimulates a response in my brain. And that response feels good.

Perhaps that flower (and beautiful buildings, art, and breathtaking natural wonders) are beautiful enough to overcome my stimuli threshold and evoke a response in me—but it's not enough to evoke it in my husband. And perhaps HSPs have a lower beauty threshold than other people. Maybe this is why we are so moved when we absorb art or nature.

---

[2] Source: http://www.biology-online.org/biology-forum/about20113.html

Aging, inevitability, and the loss of uniqueness

When I was a young kid, I remember wondering why women on TV and in movies would make jokes about lying about their age or not wanting to admit their age. I thought it was so stupid; who cares how old you are? I completely, totally did not comprehend why it was a bad thing to admit your age as an adult woman. I told myself that I would never be like that.

Well, now that I've been on the wrong side of 30 for a while, I get it. For me, the age hesitation is mainly because *I can't believe how old I am*! How did this happen? When did I become old!? Also, I don't want people to judge me or think of me differently once they know my age.

Now that I can see my physical evidence of aging, I feel like my entire identity is changed. For my first 29 years, part of my identity was "young person." So many things accompanied that youth: I could blame things on being young and naive, I could expect to be looked at a certain way by the opposite (or same) sex, and I was treated like I was fun and full of life with a big future. Then, suddenly, that part of the identity I knew my entire life was gone. I can no longer list "young" in my personal adjectives. I am expected to act the way a 30-whatever woman is supposed to act;

continuing to act like a young person is gauche and embarrassing.

Dr. Aron says that we HSPs may be more aware of the subtle changes that happen to us as we age, because, of course, we are just really aware of everything. The first thing I noticed around age 30 was my face: one day, I realized my skin didn't have a *glow* to it—it looked dull. The crazy thing is, I never realized there was *ever* a glow, until it was gone! Suddenly, I understood the phrase, "youthful glow." And just as suddenly, all the products I'd ever seen advertised for fighting aging made sense—I was now the target market for the aging cosmetic products I'd formerly rolled my eyes at.

Then there is the cynical knowledge that it's all downhill from here. I found my first gray hair and it terrified me. There it was—irrefutable evidence that I'm getting old. I will continue to get more gray hairs until it's all gray. The best I ever looked or felt has already happened. That was the peak. Now, everything is downhill. (Anticipatory grief, right?)

Jim is older than I am, but he doesn't share any of these thoughts and concerns. None of this bothers him. He figures, "Why worry about something I can't change?" I wish I felt that way.

He also said something cool: "Although your physical appearance might change or decline, you become a more interesting person when you get older because you've been through more. That's something to look forward to."

That's nice. But of course, aging leads to the Great Inevitability, and isn't that the root of it all? Aging leads to our eventual death. Death is scary.

But enough about that. How does this all relate to uniqueness?

Dr. Aron says that most HSPs "find it important to be unique. The stages at the beginning and end of life are very confining in that regard. **That inevitability can take away one's sense of individuality.**" [3]

I *do* find it important to feel unique. I guess it boils down to a fear of being similar to everyone else. If I'm not unique, then what am I? If I am like everyone else, who am I?

Let's look on the positive side of being an HSP who is getting older!

Dr. Aron points out that because we HSPs are detail-oriented, we are more likely to *age well*. We'll save money, have insurance, and follow our doctor's orders: get exercise and eat well. So that's good.

---

[3] Source: http://www.hsperson.com/pages/2Nov07.htm

She also says we tend to get more sensitive as we age.

Oh. Great.

Empathy for sport disappointments

During the 2014 World Cup, I watched the Brazil v. Chile game on TV, which ended in penalty kicks. It was down to one player: if he missed the goal, Chile would lose and be out of the tournament.

Before the kick, the player gave the referee a quick smile when he was handed the ball. It seemed like a nervous, sincere smile. It was endearing to me. I instantly liked the guy.

Then he kicked and **the ball hit the post and missed the goal.** It was over.

The next shot of his face—oh. It hit me in the heart. He looked stunned. Like he couldn't believe what just happened. Witnessing it made me so sad for the guy that I had tears in my eyes.

I don't know how these athletes handle so much pressure. They train their entire lives and the World Cup is the culmination of their entire sporting career. Then it came down to one moment, one action, and his kick lost it all for his team and his country.

If I was that guy, I'd think about that kick every single day, analyzing everything I could have done differently.

I've always been moved by emotional sports moments. If I watch highlights of a tournament— even in a sport I don't follow—my eyes often fill with tears.

When the Japanese team won the women's soccer World Cup in 2011, only a few months after the devastating tsunami, how could you not be moved? Even if you didn't care about soccer?

When one of my favorite players on my favorite hockey team retired after a long career, I sobbed my eyes out while watching his retirement ceremony.

Something about sport touches me. It's the passion and effort that athletes put into their performance. The fact that people are working together, earnestly, toward a shared goal. They are trying so hard. They want it *so* bad. How can you not feel their pain and joy?

How to explain being an HSP to your partner

Discovering that you are highly sensitive can be a life-changing realization. It's natural to want to share this new information with the most important people in your life. But it's often not easy to explain the concept to others, especially those who are skeptical of "self-diagnoses."

I've created this section to **outline** how I would explain HSP to my partner for the first time, if I had the chance to do it all over again.

_____

I just discovered something called Highly Sensitive People (HSPs), and I think I am one. I want to explain what it means because it is important to me.

Imagine if you experienced every smell, sound, and emotion ten times more intensely. That's being highly sensitive.

I know that the phrase Highly Sensitive Person might sound negative—like people who cry a lot, get offended over little things, and are overly dramatic. But that's not what it is. HSPs have "sensory processing sensitivity," which means we process the stimulus around us at a deeper, more intense level than others.

Discovering I am highly sensitive has changed the way I see myself. Instead of wishing I was different and wondering why I can't be "normal," I realize that I'm not weird or wrong. This is such a relief. It's a huge weight off my shoulders and helps me accept myself for the first time in my life.

And you—being a person who cares about me—I hope you will come along on this journey with me, since it will make me happy to know you care enough to try to understand.

Being sensitive means being more aware of everything around you—physical surroundings, other people, and, yes, emotions. Sensitivity doesn't mean weakness; that is a common misperception. Sensitive means insightful and observant, and I really identify with those traits.

Here are some aspects of Highly Sensitive People that you may have noticed in me:

- We think deeply. It can take us a long time to make a decision because we are carefully weighing all options. We hate making mistakes.

- We feel empathy for other people and creatures very strongly, sometimes as if their pain is our own.

- We may be bothered by physical discomforts, like temperature, uncomfortable furniture, and lighting, and we can't stop thinking about these bothers until they are resolved.

- We may be easily startled by sudden or loud sounds.

- We often feel a strong connection to animals.

- We are conscientious and aware of others' moods and emotions.

- We may be deeply moved by music, nature, or art.

- We don't like having many things to do at once and can feel overwhelmed easily.

- We don't like violent or gory movies or TV.

- We are often introverted (but not always).

And if you aren't convinced that being highly sensitive is a real thing—here are a few more examples:

Imagine you accidentally cut yourself, and you felt pain. Then imagine that someone else had the same injury. They might feel that pain differently than you.

We might not all feel things the same.

Okay. Now imagine you are walking down the street and you smell dog poop or rotting garbage. You don't think, "Hmm, how do I feel about that?" Instead, you have an instant, strong, negative reaction. This is what it is like to be highly sensitive. We have instant, strong reactions to things. We cannot stop or control a gut feeling. We do not decide to be more or less sensitive just like people don't *decide* that poop stinks!

(For introverted HSPs) And you know how you love to go to parties, go to the bar, and hang out with people? Well, I don't like to do those things frequently. My desire to not do those things is just as valid as your desire to do them. Neither desire is wrong. Hopefully we can find a compromise so both of our needs are met.

All I ask is that you take these things into consideration. Your understanding of HSP is very important to me. I'm happy to have learned this about myself, and hope you are, too.

It's hard to predict how your partner will react to this initial conversation. You may find that he or she needs time to process this new information, or perhaps it clicks *right away and answers many questions for them. Either way, it's likely that this new understanding will serve to improve your relationship as you work on compromise and happiness for both of you.*

The importance of kindred spirits

The first time I heard the phrase *kindred spirit* was in the popular *Anne of Green Gables* TV series from the mid-1980s, which was adapted from the L.M. Montgomery novels. The character of Anne Shirley used the term *kindred spirits* to talk about intimate friends, people with whom who she felt she could bare her soul. She held these people dear to her heart and was fiercely loyal to them.

Susan Cain, author of the best-selling introvert book *Quiet*, once said that when she is at a networking event, she is searching for just one kindred spirit. There is usually at least one at every event. These are people you want to know better, people with whom you connect, have chemistry, and want to stay in contact.

We go through life, collecting kindred spirits—people we feel connected to in our heart.

This rings true for me.

I never had many close friends at once. I usually have maybe one or two good friends. Of course, I have more *casual* friends, but not kindred spirits. There are people I like and think are nice, good people, but I don't have that deep connection with them.

The older I get, the more important it is to have that connection. When I have a great conversation with someone, I feel like I'm on a high—almost giddy. Emotionally and mentally fulfilled.

HSPs—because we have so much empathy and are good listeners—tend to be fiercely loyal friends. When I have a kindred spirit in my life, I'm not going to let them go. When I moved across the country, there was no way I was going to let my best friendship fade away, even though my friend pessimistically joked that it would. I wouldn't let it happen; it meant too much to me.

On the other hand, it's okay to let go of friendships that are not with kindred spirits.

Let me explain. Perhaps there are people in your life you consider friends, but when you really think about it, you don't actually enjoy being around them. Maybe over the years you have both changed—which is okay! People change! It is okay to let go of friends or acquaintances who do not add anything to your life (or vice versa—maybe you don't add anything to their life, either).

It sounds cold to say that you should let go of people you don't gain anything from. But honestly, what is friendship? Why waste energy and time with people with whom you don't have a connection? (Especially if they are toxic or harming your happiness in some way.) It doesn't mean there is anything wrong with either of you—you're just moving in different directions.

Having kindred spirit friends who can meet your emotional needs is crucial to an HSP. If you've ever felt alone or lonely in your life, I'm willing to bet you were missing at least one kindred spirit who could be there for you—one person with whom you felt a true camaraderie and deep connection.

My deepest feelings and emotions come out with people I connect with because it feels **safe**. With kindred spirits, I know that person cares and won't judge me, or vice versa. There are no ulterior motives. We will be loyal because we share the same care for each other.

Another cool thing about kindred spirits is that they usually reciprocate your excitement about having found you as a friend, too.

If you find a friend who is also a kindred spirit, consider yourself lucky and don't let them go.

How can you meet other HSPs, and, hopefully, kindred spirits?

Here are a few tips on how to meet conscientious, good listeners with whom you can share a deep, meaningful connection—people like you!

Meetup.com: Search for HSP Meetups or Introvert Meetups (if that applies to you). If there aren't any such groups in your area, try searching for activities that are likely to attract introverts and HSPs, like meditation groups or book clubs. Or, you could start a new group!

Reddit: To commiserate with like-minded people online, try the HSP subreddit at reddit.com/r/hsp.

Should you tell people that you are an HSP?

Think of a time you tried to explain high sensitivity to someone who'd never heard of it before. Maybe it was a friend, family member, or even a co-worker.

As you are talking, you can tell from their face that **they aren't buying it**.

You might get the following responses:

"What is the science behind HSP? Has it been proven?"
"Sometimes you just gotta suck it up and have a thick skin. Life is tough."

What they are really saying is: "I don't believe you. This sounds like a made-up excuse to get attention and special treatment."

This may lead you, the HSP, to feel:
Embarrassed,
marginalized,
narcissistic,
defensive, and
bothersome.

Then, after feeling all those emotions, I get a little irritated. It's not very nice for them to ignore my feelings and life experiences. In fact, it's quite rude and closed-minded.

We've all taken different paths to get where we are. We don't know what someone else's life has been like. If someone confided in me that they had some struggle, illness, or personality trait that I'd never heard of, I hope that my first response would not be, "I don't believe you."

Look, I know it's natural for people to question concepts that seem foreign or weird to them. All I'm asking is that people do it a teeny bit less.

If you tell a closed-minded person about high sensitivity, you run the risk of them judging you negatively. You can't change everyone's views. I personally do not tell most friends—and definitely not co-workers—that I am highly sensitive. It seems too personal, and I don't need the judgment from them. Unless they seem like open-minded, accepting people, I don't want to risk it.

However, if I know someone who seems like they might understand—a "—I might tell them. Just because it would be cool to have another person in my life who understood.

Parenting tips for introverted HSPs with kids

Parenting is a tough job—period. But imagine facing the demanding and chaotic challenges of parenthood when you're easily overstimulated and overwhelmed—a situation that occurs naturally because kids have energy and curiosity. That's the predicament faced by parents who happen to be introverted HSPs.

For them, having peaceful moments in which to reenergize is as crucial as water and air.

If we ignore our need for solitude and inner reflection, our mental well-being can suffer. We may even lash out in frustration due to sensory overwhelm, creating an emotionally charged household. Children will absorb that stress and tension that surrounds them. That's not good.

And of course, there's the guilt. The solitude we require for our own needs? That could be quality time spent with the little ones.

But highly sensitive, introverted moms and dads can thrive at the parenting game—IF they have a strategy. How? By planning ahead to ensure they have the time they require to recharge. By practicing self-care, parents can be more present and energized during family time.

Here are some tips for highly sensitive, introverted parents—especially those with non-introverted, non-sensitive spouses.

1. **Give yourself permission** to have alone time. Your kids rely on you for stability and balance, and you can't provide that if you're overwhelmed or irritable. Don't feel guilty for making sure you're the best *you* for your kids.

2. **Take a mini-retreat**. Just you. Whether it's once a week, once a month, or once a year, take a half day (or longer, if you can) to do anything you want, alone. Read for hours at a bookstore or coffee shop. Get a massage. Take a long walk. Work on your novel. Whatever you want.

3. **Schedule recharge time every day. Don't neglect it.** How about this: after everyone is asleep, engage in a quiet project or activity (not social media!) for 30 minutes to an hour—like writing, reading, doing a crossword, or giving yourself a pedicure.

4. **Or try a "room hour."** At a certain time of the day—say, after lunch—the kids go to their

room(s) for one hour. Tell the kids that this is a special time where everyone gets to recharge alone and do whatever they want. For the parent, this hour can restore calm and patience that may have worn thin earlier in the day.

5. **Use headphones** to listen to white noise or peaceful sounds if the ambient noise in your house is getting to you. (But, obviously, don't ignore your kids).

6. When planning outings and family vacations or trips, **ensure that you haven't scheduled too many "social" days** in the week before and after the trip.

7. Marriage and partnership is about **compromise**, of course. If your partner is an extrovert, you *will* have to engage in draining social activities, because that is what energizes your partner. Compensate by **alternating who gets to choose activities**. If there is a day full of socializing, compensate with a day of doing nothing.

8. Enforce a rule that only **one person can speak at a time at the dinner table**. Pitched as a family game, it can keep the kids happy while calming chaotic mealtimes.

9. **Don't ignore the voice in your head that says you need a break.** Leave the room if you need

to. Even if it's just for five minutes.

10. **Share your interests with your kids** so you can spend time together in ways you enjoy. Try reading books, gardening, or watching movies together. Similarly, **pay attention to and accept introverted and highly sensitive traits in your children**. Do you like to take short breaks from parties? Or get grumpy when there's too much going on around you? Your child may feel the same way! Your understanding can make a world of difference to helping your little human thrive and accept who they are.

Becoming a parent doesn't mean that HSPs and introverts should neglect their personal needs. When you are refreshed and energized, you can be a better parent and role model. And it's healthy for your kids to learn that taking occasional time-outs and balancing energy with calmness and peacefulness can be a *good* thing.

Conclusion

While reading this book, were there moments where you thought: *Wow, that is totally me?*

If so, then I have succeeded.

For more on HSPs, please check out my blog and podcast at highlysensitiveperson.net.

Get your bonuses!

Head over to highlysensitiveperson.net/bonus to pick up these extras:

- **A mega-list of products I love for HSPs & introverts**. From office gadgets to books to gifts for others, here is a big ol' list of items that can make life a little bit more comfortable.

- **A colorful, PDF mini-ebook of my top travel tips for HSPs.** I love to travel, but being easily overwhelmed means that I have to take some precautions when traveling that others don't. I reveal my tips on traveling (and traveling long-term), as well as why travel is good for HSPs.

- **A list of my top 5 favorite HSP podcast episodes.** These are the most helpful, thought-provoking episodes of my Highly Sensitive Person podcast.

About the author

Learning about being a Highly Sensitive Person (and introvert) changed Kelly's life; she is dedicated to helping others gain that same knowledge and self-acceptance. Kelly blogs at highlysensitiveperson.net and hosts the Highly Sensitive Person podcast. She is a writer based in Southern California.

Acknowledgments

The following people were a huge help to me. They assisted with editing, advice, support, and encouragement. Thank you!

Jim Caceres, Jenny and Lewis Smith, Valerie Chin, Julie Velky, Jerrie Pelser, Shanna Trenholm, Rob Dix, and a special mega thank you to Mish Slade.

Made in the USA
Middletown, DE
10 May 2020